Little RIDDLERS

Lincolnshire

Edited By Allie Jones

First published in Great Britain in 2018 by:

Young Writers
Remus House
Coltsfoot Drive
Peterborough
PE2 9BF
Telephone: 01733 890066
Website: www.youngwriters.co.uk

All Rights Reserved
Book Design by Ashley Janson
© Copyright Contributors 2018
SB ISBN 978-1-78896-492-0
Printed and bound in the UK by BookPrintingUK
Website: www.bookprintinguk.com
YB0362BZ

FOREWORD

Dear Reader,

Are you ready to get your thinking caps on to puzzle your way through this wonderful collection?

Young Writers' Little Riddlers competition set out to encourage young writers to create their own riddles. Their answers could be whatever or whoever their imaginations desired; from people to places, animals to objects, food to seasons. Riddles are a great way to further the children's use of poetic expression, including onomatopoeia and similes, as well as encourage them to 'think outside the box' by providing clues without giving the answer away immediately.

All of us here at Young Writers believe in the importance of inspiring young children to produce creative writing, including poetry, and we feel that seeing their own riddles in print will keep that creative spirit burning brightly and proudly.

We hope you enjoy riddling your way through this book as much as we enjoyed reading all the entries.

CONTENTS

Althorpe & Keadby Primary School, Keadby

Emily Frances Clay (7)	1
Lilly Sophia Webster (6)	2
Lilly Johnson (6)	3
Roxanna May Quinn (7)	4
Alfie Lee Rusling (7)	5
Brody Maclean (7)	6
Matthew Tong (7)	7
Kelsey Melissa Davidson (7)	8
Katelyn Louise Padbury (7)	9
Libby Fowles (7)	10
Lucas Wall (6)	11
Dylan White (6)	12

Browns CE Primary School, Horbling

Leo Charles Silvermann (6)	13
Ella-Rose Mai Walker (7)	14
Amelia Rose McCormack (6)	15
Finley David Craig (7)	16
Jorgie Marsters (6)	17
Jack Martin (6)	18
Ruben Jacob Godbold (6)	19
Frankie Atkins (5)	20
Oliver Slaughter (6)	21
Benji Morris (6)	22
Eden May McPherson (6)	23
Mason Finlay Atkins (6)	24
Ava Catherine Diston (5)	25
Oakley John Skilton (6)	26
Millie Walsh (7)	27

East Halton Primary School, East Halton

Ellie-May West (6)	28
Charlie Almond (6)	29
Fredrick Cawkwell (6)	30

Grantham Preparatory School, Grantham

Pippa Jackson (6)	31
Anna Smith (7)	32
Austen Ebbins (7)	33
Matthew Hancocks (6)	34
Christopher Manners (6)	35
Enya Lucia Mellor (7)	36
Thomas Roscoe (6)	37
Eva May Kirk (7)	38
Finley Schwartz (7)	39

Killingholme Primary School, South Killingholme

Jessica Mersom (6)	40
Casey-Leigh Hartshorn (6)	41
Jasmne Gregory (6)	42
Harvey Brisby (7)	43
Chloe Rose Johnson (6)	44
Alana Elizabeth Johnson (6)	45
Harry Godley (7)	46
Sophia Watson (6)	47
Alyssa Walker (6)	48

Lincoln Gardens Primary School, Scunthorpe

Sami Goodarzy (7)	49
Catriona Stewart Dodds (6)	50
Alexander Forrest (7)	51
Amy Wigham (7)	52
Ella Marie Taylor (7)	53
Ruby Larby (6)	54
Olivia Taylor (6)	55
Lacey Greenall (6)	56
Daisie-Rae Watson (7)	57
Khair Mohammad (6)	58
Heidi Jennifer Ling (6)	59
Alesha Kilmore (7)	60
Lily Rose Jackson (7)	61
Jake Gallagher (7)	62
Edie Holt (6)	63
Lewis Clark (6)	64
Simran Kaur (7)	65
Jensen Bee (7)	66
Byron McKenna (5)	67
Evie Rose (6)	68
Nikodem Szwab (6)	69
Charlotte Wheatley (7)	70
Katie Grace Cheyne (6)	71
Jasmine Godfrey (6)	72
Curtis Barlow (6)	73
Max Allman (5)	74
Thomas Bancroft (6)	75
Grace Louise Davies (6)	76
Reuben James Stapleton (6)	77
Tyler Walker (6)	78
Levi Presten (6)	79
Summer Musgrave (6)	80
Harry Dean Petrow (7)	81
Lillie Kathleen May Turner (6)	82
Aryana Thompson (6)	83
Lacey May Lyon (7)	84
Oliver Dean (6)	85
Luka-Archie Christopher-Cook (6)	86
Henry Johnson (7)	87
Sapphire Dawn Ayre (6)	88
Kassidi Garrod (5)	89
Maeve Altoft (6)	90
Abby Jackson (6)	91
Kody Garrod (7)	92
Dexter Doyle (7)	93
Harry Finch (6)	94
Layla Swift (6)	95
Leah Milne (7)	96
Annabel Foster (7)	97
Keeley Fraser-Raynes (7)	98

Macaulay Primary Academy, Grimsby

Dannie-Louise Hall (7)	99
Grayson Morris Green (6)	100
Emanuel Albu (6)	102
Farzan Salehi (7)	103
Ciaran Michael Holness (6)	104
Layla Fogarty (7)	105
Escarla Harrison (6)	106
Roxy Louise Walden (6)	107
Mckenzie Ashton (6)	108
Leo Wardle (6)	109
Maycie Ellis (7)	110

Queen Mary Avenue Infant School, Cleethorpes

Konal Bennett (6)	111
Lexie Newport (6)	112
Ivy Marie Rodgers-Gibbs (7)	113
Macauley Forbes (6)	114
Chloe Binley (7)	115
Kellen Alfred Marriott (6)	116
Tyler Padbury (7)	117
Alfie Robertson (6)	118
Tyler Campbell (7)	119
Gracie-Mai Jeanine Younger (7)	120
Brody Hollinghworth (7)	121
Maisie Melinda Mary Marshall (6)	122
Alan Zyamunt (7)	123
Joshua Farrar (7)	124

Laila Campbell (6)	125
Brogan Lawson (6)	126
Callum Hooper (6)	127
Dougie Brennan (6)	128
Ewan Conchar (7)	129
Jayden Webster-Olley (7)	130
Amelia Erin Rayne-Beau Byram (7)	131
Riley Noble (6)	132
Bailey Jay Taylor-Dunham (7)	133

Seathorne Primary School, Skegness

Martha Piercey (7)	134
Kayden Hodgson (7)	135
Lexie Frost (7)	136
Jaxon Young (6)	137
Emily Boyle (7)	138
Nico Gedney (6)	139
Charlie Webb (7)	140
Ellie Manley (7)	141
Evie Lily Beale (7)	142
Summer Louise Turner (7)	143
Lilli Mitchell (6)	144
Kainan Brooks (7)	145
Grace Gathercole (7)	146
Jacob Blythe (7)	147
Borys Chojnacki (6)	148
Maisie Ladds (7)	149
Lilith Scarlet Thompson (7)	150
Riley Hale (6)	151
Amelia Rose Holmes (7)	152
Lilly-Mai Allan (6)	153
Lily-Beth Ellen Brader (7)	154
Chloe Carey (7)	155
Jacobi-Joe Welbourn (7)	156
Noah Howe (7)	157
Kyra Feeley (6)	158
Daniel Luke Stephenson (7)	159
Chelsie Lyn Taylor (7)	160
Cooper Rolfe (6)	161
Brooklyn Whitworth (6)	162
Alfie Thomson (7)	163

Wyatt Senior (7)	164
Sophie Clarke (6)	165
Preston Wilkinson (6)	166
Jayden Dylan Senanayake-Andrew (7)	167
Teyen Wood (6)	168

Wragby Primary School, Wragby

Maisie Wallis (7)	169
David-Malakai Kuyava (6)	170
Daniel Blood (7)	171
Gracie Lowe (6)	172
Noah Pearce (6)	173
Sophie Olivia Millington (6)	174
Ben Spencer (7)	175
Evie Deans (6)	176
Amy Chamberlain (6)	177
Archie Mark Angél Rushin (6)	178
Riley Joseph Spittles (6)	179
Zac Garth (6)	180
Thomas Blyth (6)	181
Taya Nganga (6)	182
Thomas Skellern (7)	183
Charlotte Wallis (7)	184
Phoebe Cooper (7)	185
Madeline Wade (7)	186
Ethen Hook-Bingham (6)	187

THE POEMS

Let's Live

I am made out of smooth, white wood.
I have beautiful, wooden dolls inside me.
I have sparkly, clean windows on me.
I don't have four, black wheels.
I have a smooth, pointy roof.
I've got colourful furniture inside me.
What am I?

Answer: A doll's house.

Emily Frances Clay (7)
Althorpe & Keadby Primary School, Keadby

Swinging In The Trees

I have soft, brown fur that's fluffy.
I am soft and furry.
I squeeze bananas out of the peel.
You can sleep at night with me.
I like swinging on a spiky tree like a snake.
I have sparkly fur when I'm in front of the sun.
What am I?

Answer: A monkey.

Lilly Sophia Webster (6)
Althorpe & Keadby Primary School, Keadby

Seashells

I have soft, curly hair.
My eyes are as blue as the sky.
I have a smooth, dull body.
I'm a playful toy.
I have lots of beautiful and colourful outfits.
I have a beautiful, pink crown on my head.
What am I?

Answer: A mermaid.

Lilly Johnson (6)
Althorpe & Keadby Primary School, Keadby

Loving Pet

I'm very massive, brown and soft.
You can cuddle me.
I've got a red, sparkly tongue.
It's a long, fat tongue.
I'm like cold, plastic things.
I have big, cuddly fur.
What am I?

Answer: A dog teddy.

Roxanna May Quinn (7)
Althorpe & Keadby Primary School, Keadby

Machine

I am shaped like a block.
I have friends that are different.
I can move with my tall, thin legs.
I can't die.
I am colourful and rough.
I have shiny, black eyes.
What am I?

Answer: A Roblox.

Alfie Lee Rusling (7)
Althorpe & Keadby Primary School, Keadby

Fast

I am black, shiny metal.
I can be spun fast.
I have three metal corners.
I am as blue as the sky.
I am super fast.
When you are bored you can play with me.
What am I?

Answer: A *fidget spinner*.

Brody Maclean (7)
Althorpe & Keadby Primary School, Keadby

Slow

I have a long, green body.
I go as slow as a slug.
I go into a cocoon.
I turn into something beautiful.
I fly with slow wings.
I lay eggs on leaves.
What am I?

Answer: A caterpillar.

Matthew Tong (7)
Althorpe & Keadby Primary School, Keadby

Hatchling

I can move in my egg.
I am soft and cuddly.
I have dark purple fur.
I have shiny, colourful eyes.
I can sing birthday songs.
I am as simple as a bike.
What am I?

Answer: A Hatchimal.

Kelsey Melissa Davidson (7)
Althorpe & Keadby Primary School, Keadby

Jack

I have a long, fluffy tail.
I am as black as the night sky.
I live in a big stable.
I have long eyes.
I can eat grass.
I can carry people on my back.
What am I?

Answer: A donkey.

Katelyn Louise Padbury (7)
Althorpe & Keadby Primary School, Keadby

Plastic

I have long, black hair.
I'm made of hard plastic.
I have big, pink boots.
I wear a rainbow dress.
You play with me.
You make me look beautiful.
What am I?

Answer: A Barbie.

Libby Fowles (7)
Althorpe & Keadby Primary School, Keadby

Pedal Power

I have two big, black wheels.
I'm fast.
You ride on me.
I have a comfy, black seat.
I've got a blue and white frame.
I'm as fast as a car.
What am I?

Answer: A bike.

Lucas Wall (6)
Althorpe & Keadby Primary School, Keadby

Blast-Off

I'm speedy like a motorbike.
I'll play with you.
I can go into black space.
I like black space.
I have a boost.
Some people ride in me.
What am I?

Answer: A rocket.

Dylan White (6)
Althorpe & Keadby Primary School, Keadby

The Big, Nice Giant

I have horns on my back,
And I have a pointy, sharp nose.
I feel grumpy and I feel grisly.
I roar and I grumble.
I run away from my enemies,
Because they are terrifying and hungry.
I eat too much.
My horns protect me,
From big rocks blocking my way.
What am I?

Answer: A rhino.

Leo Charles Silvermann (6)
Browns CE Primary School, Horbling

The Outside Weather

When you are inside,
I love to play in the beautiful outdoors.
My arms are all different.
I fall from high places.
I'm wet and cold,
But warm on the inside.
When you celebrate, I love to play.
I come out once a year.
What am I?

Answer: A snowflake.

Ella-Rose Mai Walker (7)
Browns CE Primary School, Horbling

The Interesting Thing

I sit in silence,
But I have lots to say.
I'm long and short,
And all different sizes.
I know everything.
You need to carry me.
I open and close.
I like to travel around but I can't walk.
What am I?

Answer: A book.

Amelia Rose McCormack (6)
Browns CE Primary School, Horbling

I Light Up With Light

I like to bang,
And I like to crackle.
I like to whistle loudly at night-time.
I have got beautiful colours all night long.
I boom in the night.
I come out when you celebrate.
I go up high.
What am I?

Answer: A firework.

Finley David Craig (7)
Browns CE Primary School, Horbling

A Long Time Underground

I'm really smooth.
I'm beautifully brown.
I've been underground for a million years.
I can be anything.
I can be different sizes.
I can be from a different dinosaur.
What am I?

Answer: A fossil.

Jorgie Marsters (6)
Browns CE Primary School, Horbling

The Hunter

I like to hunt where people can't see me.
I am a terrifying, hungry carnivore.
I come in different shapes.
I am a predator.
I have sharp talons.
I scream loudly.
What am I?

Answer: A bird of prey.

Jack Martin (6)
Browns CE Primary School, Horbling

What Am I?

Once a year my hair falls off.
I am tall and I change colour over the year.
I swish in the wind.
I have hard, tough skin.
If the wind blows too hard I will fall over.
What am I?

Answer: A tree.

Ruben Jacob Godbold (6)
Browns CE Primary School, Horbling

The Lovings

They are helpful and pretty.
They like to talk.
They like to snuggle up.
They take me to exciting places.
They help me learn.
They play with me.
Who are they?

Answer: My family.

Frankie Atkins (5)
Browns CE Primary School, Horbling

What Am I?

I have a black nose.
I feel furry.
I have a scary growl.
I can be white, red or brown.
I have sharp, pointy teeth.
I live in a scary, dark cave.
What am I?

Answer: A bear.

Oliver Slaughter (6)
Browns CE Primary School, Horbling

Burning

I am big and tough.
I am scary.
I have sharp teeth.
If you come near me I might burn you.
I fly with my giant wings.
I am a strong fighter.
What am I?

Answer: A dragon.

Benji Morris (6)
Browns CE Primary School, Horbling

What Am I?

I have pointy teeth,
That cut through my prey.
I feel scaly.
I growl angrily.
I stomp loudly.
I hunt silently.
I am no longer here.
What am I?

Answer: A dinosaur.

Eden May McPherson (6)
Browns CE Primary School, Horbling

In The Jungle

Maybe I am red.
Maybe I am small.
I sound like the sea.
Sometimes I bite.
I wiggle through the grass.
Maybe I have scratches on me.
What am I?

Answer: A snake.

Mason Finlay Atkins (6)
Browns CE Primary School, Horbling

What Am I?

I have a long tail.
I feel furry.
I might be black and white.
I hiss when I am angry.
I walk on four legs.
I drink milk and water.
What am I?

Answer: A cat.

Ava Catherine Diston (5)
Browns CE Primary School, Horbling

What Am I?

I have brown spots.
I have horns.
I am quiet.
I walk on four legs.
I eat leaves off the long trees.
I have long legs.
What am I?

Answer: A giraffe.

Oakley John Skilton (6)
Browns CE Primary School, Horbling

What Can You Buy For A Penny?

I am colourful.
I can be big or small.
I am sweet or sour.
I can't walk.
I make you hyper.
You really want me.
What am I?

Answer: A sweet.

Millie Walsh (7)
Browns CE Primary School, Horbling

Goldy

I was born without a voice,
I had no choice.
I die without complaining.
I want to get out of that bowl,
With all of my soul.
I am entertaining.
What am I?

Answer: A goldfish.

Ellie-May West (6)
East Halton Primary School, East Halton

My Healthy Snack

I am round.
I taste sweet and juicy.
My colour is bright.
I am a fruit.
You peel me.
Sometimes I have pips.
What am I?

Answer: An orange.

Charlie Almond (6)
East Halton Primary School, East Halton

Automotive

I am big and small.
I come in lots of colours.
I need fuel to go.
I can go anywhere.
I go fast or slow.
What am I?

Answer: A car.

Fredrick Cawkwell (6)
East Halton Primary School, East Halton

Bouncing Through The Green

I am very fluffy,
And I have long ears.
I have a very fluffy tail.
In French, I am called le lapin.
I bounce through the green grass.
My favourite foods are carrots and lettuce.
I have a very twitchy nose.
My predator is a fox.
I do not like being in a small cage,
It's too cramped.
What am I?

Answer: A rabbit.

Pippa Jackson (6)
Grantham Preparatory School, Grantham

The Cold

I stand still.
I am made out of snow,
And I have a carrot as a nose.
I come at Christmas,
And children like to play with me.
I am in a film.
I am freezing to touch.
I melt in the sun.
What am I?

Answer: A snowman.

Anna Smith (7)
Grantham Preparatory School, Grantham

I Am Endangered

I eat leaves and twigs.
I am black and white.
I have a long snout.
I am a good swimmer.
I can live up to 30 years.
I live in South America.
Tigers like to eat me.
I am 150cm tall.
What am I?

Answer: A tapir.

Austen Ebbins (7)
Grantham Preparatory School, Grantham

Thorn Power!

I smell beautiful.
I come in different colours.
You can pick me,
And put me in a vase.
I am a type of flower.
I have thorns on my stem.
I am often given on Valentine's Day.
What am I?

Answer: A rose.

Matthew Hancocks (6)
Grantham Preparatory School, Grantham

What Am I?

My tail is longer than my body.
I am endangered.
I stink fight.
I live in Madagascar.
I eat leaves, fruit and bark.
A group of me is called a troop.
What am I?

Answer: A lemur.

Christopher Manners (6)
Grantham Preparatory School, Grantham

What Am I?

I am very stripy.
I hunt for my prey.
I am a feline.
I live in the rainforest.
I am big and strong.
I am a wild animal.
What am I?

Answer: A tiger.

Enya Lucia Mellor (7)
Grantham Preparatory School, Grantham

Spiky Head

I have two horns.
I am grey.
I live in Africa.
I chase other animals.
I am heavy.
I am very strong.
What am I?

Answer: A rhino.

Thomas Roscoe (6)
Grantham Preparatory School, Grantham

Juicy

I am red.
I have pips.
I am shaped like a love heart.
I have a stem.
I love cream.
What am I?

Answer: A strawberry.

Eva May Kirk (7)
Grantham Preparatory School, Grantham

What Am I?

I am black and white.
I sleep all day,
And hug my prey.
What am I?

Answer: A panda.

Finley Schwartz (7)
Grantham Preparatory School, Grantham

The Hopping Creature

I like carrots.
I live in a cage.
I am cute.
I am fuzzy.
I am woolly.
I have sharp teeth.
What am I?

Answer: A pet rabbit.

Jessica Mersom (6)
Killingholme Primary School, South Killingholme

My Pet

I have a lot of fur.
I wiggle my tail.
I have four legs.
I have sharp claws.
I hunt for bones.
What am I?

Answer: A dog.

Casey-Leigh Hartshorn (6)
Killingholme Primary School, South Killingholme

The Black And White Animal

I drink milk.
I am furry.
I have four paws.
I eat food.
I am cute.
I am black and white.
What am I?

Answer: A cat.

Jasmne Gregory (6)
Killingholme Primary School, South Killingholme

In A Forest

I eat honey.
I am brown.
I live in a cave.
I have a baby.
I can stand up.
I am big.
What am I?

Answer: A bear.

Harvey Brisby (7)
Killingholme Primary School, South Killingholme

The Little Ball Of Fluff

I miaow.
I am fluffy.
I like to play with my ball.
I like to play with string.
I am cute.
What am I?

Answer: A cat.

Chloe Rose Johnson (6)
Killingholme Primary School, South Killingholme

What Baby Am I?

I am cute.
I like milk.
I like to miaow.
I like water.
I am fluffy.
I am furry.
What am I?

Answer: A kitten.

Alana Elizabeth Johnson (6)
Killingholme Primary School, South Killingholme

Rider

I fly in the sky.
I am the fastest.
I go to places.
I am big.
I take you on holiday.
What am I?

Answer: A jet.

Harry Godley (7)
Killingholme Primary School, South Killingholme

My Pet

I love to run.
I am cuddly.
I lick.
I have a collar.
I have a tail.
What am I?

Answer: A dog.

Sophia Watson (6)
Killingholme Primary School, South Killingholme

Stripy Horse

I have black and white stripes.
I look like a horse.
I can live in a zoo.
What am I?

Answer: A zebra.

Alyssa Walker (6)
Killingholme Primary School, South Killingholme

The Furry Dream

Oh deary me, what a beautiful sight,
But if you come near I might have a bite.
When I bite and play,
Oh, it is a beautiful day.
I'm as cute as a daisy,
But can be crazy.
I love to be furry and cute all night,
I have whiskers.
I'm very small.
I eat lots of wet food.
I put you in a good mood.
What am I?

Answer: A cat.

Sami Goodarzy (7)
Lincoln Gardens Primary School, Scunthorpe

Spring Is Nice

I am very healthy,
And what comes from me is delicious.
I have red or green apples coming from me.
I am extremely still.
I let humans pick apples from my yummy place.
I have delicious, scrumptious, yummy apples.
What am I?

Answer: An apple tree.

Catriona Stewart Dodds (6)
Lincoln Gardens Primary School, Scunthorpe

Food Fun

I'm a yummy food.
You can put different toppings on me.
I've got a yummy and crunchy crust.
I can be ordered or made at home.
I come in a square or a circle box.
You can eat me by hand.
What am I?

Answer: A pizza.

Alexander Forrest (7)
Lincoln Gardens Primary School, Scunthorpe

Summer In The Sun

I am extremely tall.
I am really bushy and green.
My leaves fall off me.
I am spiky and I can hurt you.
I can give you a splinter.
I am stood still in the ground.
What am I?

Answer: A summer tree.

Amy Wigham (7)
Lincoln Gardens Primary School, Scunthorpe

A Small Animal

I have shiny whiskers.
I like to eat hard and soft food.
I'm colourful.
I like to purr loudly.
I like to lie on you.
If you pick me up I will purr in an angry way.
What am I?

Answer: A cat.

Ella Marie Taylor (7)
Lincoln Gardens Primary School, Scunthorpe

Cutie Cuddles

I have a very fluffy tail.
I don't really like people that much.
I am very, very small.
I have pink inside my ears.
I am black.
I climb stuff like big gates.
What am I?

Answer: A cat.

Ruby Larby (6)
Lincoln Gardens Primary School, Scunthorpe

Dream Big, Fluffy

I can be lots of different sizes.
I can be many different colours.
I live with humans.
I can bark.
I love to play and run,
But most of all, I love to be stroked.
What am I?

Answer: A dog.

Olivia Taylor (6)
Lincoln Gardens Primary School, Scunthorpe

Long Legs

I am very tall.
I am very furry.
I am healthy.
I am as tall as a tree.
I have a big, long tail.
I have small, fluffy ears.
I am as spotty as can be.
What am I?

Answer: A giraffe.

Lacey Greenall (6)
Lincoln Gardens Primary School, Scunthorpe

Waterling

I can be eaten.
I am a fruit.
I have seeds.
You can't eat my skin.
I am green on the outside,
But red on the inside.
I am very juicy.
What am I?

Answer: A watermelon.

Daisie-Rae Watson (7)
Lincoln Gardens Primary School, Scunthorpe

The Scary Cat

I have medium eyes.
I have a furry tail.
I have little, white whiskers.
I like to purr calmly.
I have big, furry hair.
I have a little, black nose.
What am I?

Answer: A lion.

Khair Mohammad (6)
Lincoln Gardens Primary School, Scunthorpe

My Juicy Fruit

I have yellow dots all over my body.
I have got nice, green leaves.
I have got a red body.
My body is ripe and juicy.
My leaves are really pointy.
What am I?

Answer: A strawberry.

Heidi Jennifer Ling (6)
Lincoln Gardens Primary School, Scunthorpe

Seaside Fun

I am extremely hot.
I am really windy and fun.
I am nice and relaxing.
I can make you smile.
I can make your day.
I can make you want ice cream.
What am I?

Answer: Summer.

Alesha Kilmore (7)
Lincoln Gardens Primary School, Scunthorpe

Watering

I can be eaten.
I am a fruit.
I have seeds.
You can't eat my skin.
I am very juicy.
I am green on the outside,
And red inside.
What am I?

Answer: A watermelon.

Lily Rose Jackson (7)
Lincoln Gardens Primary School, Scunthorpe

Season Power

I am really warm.
I am nice and sunny.
I am a season.
I am a nice time to go on holiday.
You won't need a coat.
You can play outside.
What am I?

Answer: Summer.

Jake Gallagher (7)
Lincoln Gardens Primary School, Scunthorpe

Spiky

I am really spiky.
When I eat I make a crunchy sound.
My nose is wet.
My tummy is soft.
I eat food with worms.
My feet are spiky.
What am I?

Answer: A hedgehog.

Edie Holt (6)
Lincoln Gardens Primary School, Scunthorpe

I Am Fierce

I have hard horns.
I am soft.
I like grass.
I live in fields.
I sometimes eat grass.
I am a herbivore.
I can break things.
What am I?

Answer: A bull.

Lewis Clark (6)
Lincoln Gardens Primary School, Scunthorpe

Stick Catcher

I'm fast and furry.
I have a brown tail.
I have long, floppy ears.
I am an animal.
I have a panda mouth.
I have sharp teeth.
What am I?

Answer: A dog.

Simran Kaur (7)
Lincoln Gardens Primary School, Scunthorpe

What Am I?

I have a swishy tail.
I have a spiky mane.
I have fast legs.
I have floppy whiskers.
I have a rough nose.
I have wriggly ears.
What am I?

Answer: A lion.

Jensen Bee (7)
Lincoln Gardens Primary School, Scunthorpe

I Have Very Big Spots

I am big and tall.
I like to eat grass.
I live in the jungle,
And it is clear.
I sometimes eat grass.
I am a carnivore.
What am I?

Answer: A giraffe.

Byron McKenna (5)
Lincoln Gardens Primary School, Scunthorpe

A Cheeky Pet

I have soft fur.
I am cute.
I like to eat rats.
I live in a beautiful house.
I sometimes snuggle up to my mum.
I am small.
What am I?

Answer: A cat.

Evie Rose (6)
Lincoln Gardens Primary School, Scunthorpe

What Am I?

I have four legs.
My head is covered in fur.
I have a furry tail.
I live in the wild.
I like roaring.
I hunt for my prey.
What am I?

Answer: A lion.

Nikodem Szwab (6)
Lincoln Gardens Primary School, Scunthorpe

Run In The Race

I love to run.
I can be big.
I have a lot of hair on my body.
I have quite big ears.
I love to jump too.
I like to race.
What am I?

Answer: A hare.

Charlotte Wheatley (7)
Lincoln Gardens Primary School, Scunthorpe

Learning How To Roar

I am extremely fluffy,
And everyone is scared of me.
I have big, sharp teeth,
To rip my prey up with.
I have a fluffy tail.
What am I?

Answer: A lion.

Katie Grace Cheyne (6)
Lincoln Gardens Primary School, Scunthorpe

Growling

I come from the zoo.
I can grow up too fast.
I am orange.
I like to run.
I have soft hair.
I have a soft, curly tail.
What am I?

Answer: A lion.

Jasmine Godfrey (6)
Lincoln Gardens Primary School, Scunthorpe

Fruity Fun

I am sometimes red or green.
I am delicious.
I can be cut into really little sticks.
I am very healthy.
I am super hard.
What am I?

Answer: An apple.

Curtis Barlow (6)
Lincoln Gardens Primary School, Scunthorpe

Bite

I have big teeth.
I am scary.
I like meat.
I live in the sea.
I sometimes bite.
I am an omnivore.
I can swim.
What am I?

Answer: A shark.

Max Allman (5)
Lincoln Gardens Primary School, Scunthorpe

I Like To Roam

I have very soft fur.
I am small.
I like to catch mice.
I live in the wild.
I sometimes hunt mice.
I am a carnivore.
What am I?

Answer: A cat.

Thomas Bancroft (6)
Lincoln Gardens Primary School, Scunthorpe

What A Pet

I have four legs.
I am very cute.
I like fish.
I live in a house with you.
I sometimes pounce for mice.
I have paws.
What am I?

Answer: A cat.

Grace Louise Davies (6)
Lincoln Gardens Primary School, Scunthorpe

Animal Fun

I am extremely fluffy.
I am black.
I am good at smelling stuff.
I am so, so good at running.
I am so, so good at turning.
What am I?

Answer: A dog.

Reuben James Stapleton (6)
Lincoln Gardens Primary School, Scunthorpe

Here I Am

I have fluffy fur.
I am fat.
I like meat.
I live in a big house.
I sometimes bark at people.
I have long legs.
What am I?

Answer: A dog.

Tyler Walker (6)
Lincoln Gardens Primary School, Scunthorpe

Here I Come

I have a tail.
I am little.
I like dog food.
I live in a home.
I sometimes jump at you.
I am called a pet.
What am I?

Answer: A dog.

Levi Presten (6)
Lincoln Gardens Primary School, Scunthorpe

Watch Out

I have lovely eyes.
I am fluffy.
I like meat.
I live in a big house.
I sometimes bark at people.
I am big.
What am I?

Answer: A dog.

Summer Musgrave (6)
Lincoln Gardens Primary School, Scunthorpe

Man's Best Friend

I have a furry body.
I can be friendly.
Police can use me.
I like to play fetch.
Some of us can perform tricks.
What am I?

Answer: A dog.

Harry Dean Petrow (7)
Lincoln Gardens Primary School, Scunthorpe

Cuddles

I am fierce.
I am furry.
I have an orange body.
I have got a stripy tail.
I eat meat.
I live in a zoo.
What am I?

Answer: A tiger.

Lillie Kathleen May Turner (6)
Lincoln Gardens Primary School, Scunthorpe

What Am I?

I have four legs.
I have a mane.
I live in a field.
I have a big body.
I make a sound.
I have a tail.
What am I?

Answer: A horse.

Aryana Thompson (6)
Lincoln Gardens Primary School, Scunthorpe

A Feline Friend

I have whiskers.
I like to purr softly.
I have a big, bushy tail.
I have pointy ears.
I have a soft tail.
What am I?

Answer: A cat.

Lacey May Lyon (7)
Lincoln Gardens Primary School, Scunthorpe

Juicy Fruit

I am juicy.
You can peel me.
I can have seeds.
I can be sour.
I am round.
I have small dimples.
What am I?

Answer: An orange.

Oliver Dean (6)
Lincoln Gardens Primary School, Scunthorpe

Man's Best Friend

I say *woof, woof*.
I can run fast.
I have floppy ears.
I wiggle my tail.
I like to go for walks.
What am I?

Answer: A dog.

Luka-Archie Christopher-Cook (6)
Lincoln Gardens Primary School, Scunthorpe

The Kicker

I have squares.
I am as round as a big face.
I have air.
You can pump me up.
You can blow me up.
What am I?

Answer: A football.

Henry Johnson (7)
Lincoln Gardens Primary School, Scunthorpe

I'm Red

I am red and very juicy.
I'm a food.
You can chop me up.
You can eat me.
I am very juicy.
What am I?

Answer: A strawberry.

Sapphire Dawn Ayre (6)
Lincoln Gardens Primary School, Scunthorpe

What Am I?

I have four legs.
I have a tail.
I have two ears.
I have fur.
I bark.
I have two eyes.
What am I?

Answer: A dog.

Kassidi Garrod (5)
Lincoln Gardens Primary School, Scunthorpe

What Is He?

I have four legs.
I live at home.
I am furry.
I like to make a sound.
I have a furry tail.
What am I?

Answer: A cat.

Maeve Altoft (6)
Lincoln Gardens Primary School, Scunthorpe

Taking Care Of People

I take care of poorly people.
I help them feel better,
And get well.
I can give medicine.
Who am I?

Answer: A doctor.

Abby Jackson (6)
Lincoln Gardens Primary School, Scunthorpe

The Ribbit

I am an animal.
I am smooth.
I can croak.
I am green.
I can hop.
I have feet.
What am I?

Answer: A frog.

Kody Garrod (7)
Lincoln Gardens Primary School, Scunthorpe

Kick The Spots

I have squares.
I am round.
I have air.
You can pump me up.
I am big.
What am I?

Answer: A football.

Dexter Doyle (7)
Lincoln Gardens Primary School, Scunthorpe

What Am I?

I have stripes.
I have a big, stripy tail.
I have sharp claws.
I eat meat.
What am I?

Answer: A tiger.

Harry Finch (6)
Lincoln Gardens Primary School, Scunthorpe

Roar

I have a tail.
I have a head.
I have legs.
I have a body.
I have fur.
What am I?

Answer: A lion.

Layla Swift (6)
Lincoln Gardens Primary School, Scunthorpe

A Long Friend

I eat grass.
I drink water.
I have a long neck.
I am yellow and brown.
What am I?

Answer: A giraffe.

Leah Milne (7)
Lincoln Gardens Primary School, Scunthorpe

I Have A Long Neck

I have a long neck.
I love eating leaves.
I have spots.
I have eyes.
What am I?

Answer: A giraffe.

Annabel Foster (7)
Lincoln Gardens Primary School, Scunthorpe

Licking

I have a tongue.
I have a tail.
I have four legs.
I have a body.
What am I?

Answer: A dog.

Keeley Fraser-Raynes (7)
Lincoln Gardens Primary School, Scunthorpe

Pretty To My Eye

I come out when it's wet,
But the sun has to be shining too.
You'll see me in the sky,
But I am not a plane.
They say if you can find my ends,
There will be treasure,
But I am not a chest.
I have a curved shape,
But I am not a banana.
I come with lots of colours,
But I am not a pack of crayons.
I'm a bow that cannot be tied.
What am I?

Answer: A rainbow.

Dannie-Louise Hall (7)
Macaulay Primary Academy, Grimsby

Boy In The Cupboard Under The Stairs

Every night I sleep in a small room,
With nothing all around me but darkness and brooms.
No one in this family seems to care,
That every night I sleep under the stairs.
Strange things happen when I get angry or upset,
Like glass disappearing that let out the pet.
Sometimes I dream about a flash of green light,
My lightning bolt-shaped scar hurts with such might.
Until this morning, when I received a magical letter,
By a brown tawny owl with a thump and a clatter.

So off on the red steam train to Hogwarts I go,
On this magical adventure with new friends and foe.
Who am I?

Answer: Harry Potter.

Grayson Morris Green (6)
Macaulay Primary Academy, Grimsby

What Am I?

I have many chairs,
But I am not a bus.
I have windows,
But I am not a car.
I can blow smoke out of the back.
I am made of metal,
But I am not a submarine.
I can reach the sky with many people.
I can fly,
But I am not a bird.
What am I?

Answer: A plane.

Emanuel Albu (6)
Macaulay Primary Academy, Grimsby

What Am I?

I look like a basketball that's a green colour.
I am a heavy fruit.
I have green skin.
I'm a fruit of the summer,
And I have black seeds in me.
Inside I am a red colour,
And I am a shape called an ellipsoid.
I am sweet.
What am I?

Answer: A watermelon.

Farzan Salehi (7)
Macaulay Primary Academy, Grimsby

Fast And Slow

I'm a three-letter word.
When driving me, use my mirrors.
Use my steering wheel to change direction.
My pedals make me go fast and slow.
I could be the colour red.
I come in different shapes and sizes.
What am I?

Answer: A car.

Ciaran Michael Holness (6)
Macaulay Primary Academy, Grimsby

Guess Who I Am

My hair is in a bun,
And I wear a bun net.
My dress is pink.
My shoes are pink and pointy.
I dance really floaty like a sugar plum fairy.
You can find me in a jewellery box,
Or a dance studio.
What am I?

Answer: A ballerina.

Layla Fogarty (7)
Macaulay Primary Academy, Grimsby

What Am I?

I've got a red tongue.
I swirl on trees.
I have patterns.
I am green.
I am like a line.
I am colourful.
I have a pipey and soft body.
Be careful, I might wrap you.
I am skinny.
What am I?

Answer: A snake.

Escarla Harrison (6)
Macaulay Primary Academy, Grimsby

Animal Power

I am very fragile.
If you touch me, I will collapse.
I am very colourful.
I am very tricky to find,
If you find me, you're very, very lucky.
I used to be a caterpillar.
What am I?

Answer: A butterfly.

Roxy Louise Walden (6)
Macaulay Primary Academy, Grimsby

Fierce

I have stripy fur.
I live in the jungle.
I am part of the cat family.
I have big, sharp teeth.
I am fierce.
What am I?

Answer: A tiger.

Mckenzie Ashton (6)
Macaulay Primary Academy, Grimsby

Noise In The Kitchen

I am quite big.
I make a noise.
I like clothes.
I get hot.
I am loud.
I keep clothes clean.
What am I?

Answer: A washing machine.

Leo Wardle (6)
Macaulay Primary Academy, Grimsby

What Am I?

I live underwater.
I am big.
I am scary.
I have a fin.
I have sharp teeth.
I have gills.
What am I?

Answer: A shark.

Maycie Ellis (7)
Macaulay Primary Academy, Grimsby

A Woodland Creature Riddle

I'm sometimes described as sly.
I'm big and fast.
I'm big and furry.
I'm furious and angry.
I am wild.
I live in a jungle.
Hunters try to find me.
I am orange.
I have a really bushy, huge tail.
I am in a magical forest.
What am I?

Answer: A fox.

Konal Bennett (6)
Queen Mary Avenue Infant School, Cleethorpes

Magical Horse

I have a flowing rainbow mane.
I am normally a white pearly colour.
I have a magical, pink, sparkly horn.
I live on a fluffy cloud.
I have rainbows on my body.
I have a fluffy tail.
I'm a magical creature.
What am I?

Answer: A unicorn.

Lexie Newport (6)
Queen Mary Avenue Infant School, Cleethorpes

Special Pet

I have four paws.
I am a dog with black, curly fur.
I have little, pointy teeth.
I like to tease cats.
I like to swim.
I like to bark.
I have an owner called Dorothy.
I went somewhere over the rainbow.
Who am I?

Answer: Toto the dog.

Ivy Marie Rodgers-Gibbs (7)
Queen Mary Avenue Infant School, Cleethorpes

Sizzler

I have scaly, colourful skin.
Some people are scared of me.
I live in the jungle.
I am poisonous.
People sometimes buy me for a lot of money.
I am lonely.
I am very tough and brave.
I have black eyes.
What am I?

Answer: A snake.

Macauley Forbes (6)
Queen Mary Avenue Infant School, Cleethorpes

Antarctic Riddle

I am black and white.
I have flippers.
I dive to get food.
I can swim but other animals like me fly.
I live in the icy, freezing Antarctic.
I eat fish that are in the water.
What am I?

Answer: A penguin.

Chloe Binley (7)
Queen Mary Avenue Infant School, Cleethorpes

Wheel Power

I pull lots of carriages.
I run on tracks.
I can come in different colours.
I am faster than a cheetah.
I am the fastest in the world.
I am pointy.
What am I?

Answer: A High City train.

Kellen Alfred Marriott (6)
Queen Mary Avenue Infant School, Cleethorpes

What Am I?

I have eight curly claws.
I have a giant head.
I live under the ocean.
I have a giant head.
I have three hearts.
I change colour.
I secrete ink.
What am I?

Answer: An octopus.

Tyler Padbury (7)
Queen Mary Avenue Infant School, Cleethorpes

The Green Giant

I have white, pointy, sharp teeth.
I hunt for lots of types of meat.
I roar extremely loudly.
I sometimes eat babies and children,
And adults as well.
What am I?

Answer: A T-rex.

Alfie Robertson (6)
Queen Mary Avenue Infant School, Cleethorpes

Land Long Ago

I am as tall as a big giraffe.
I eat juicy leaves.
I'm a herbivore.
I'm very old,
And I have a long neck.
I am a type of dinosaur.
What am I?

Answer: A diplodocus.

Tyler Campbell (7)
Queen Mary Avenue Infant School, Cleethorpes

Shiniest Power

I'm the shiniest thing you have seen.
I am a shape.
I glow in the sky.
I twinkle in the sky.
I come out at night.
I shine with the moon.
What am I?

Answer: A star.

Gracie-Mai Jeanine Younger (7)
Queen Mary Avenue Infant School, Cleethorpes

Sea Creatures

I am a red colour.
I walk sideways.
My habitat is sandy with stones and rock.
I have a hard shell,
And sharp claws.
People can eat me.
What am I?

Answer: A crab.

Brody Hollinghworth (7)
Queen Mary Avenue Infant School, Cleethorpes

Magic Riddle

I have wands and wings.
I have a sack.
I come at night-time.
I leave a penny.
I am magic.
I check teeth when they fall out.
Who am I?

Answer: *The tooth fairy.*

Maisie Melinda Mary Marshall (6)
Queen Mary Avenue Infant School, Cleethorpes

A Slippery Riddle

You can find me in the park.
I am big, lumpy and smooth.
I am in the big, lost park.
I can fit lots of people on me.
I have some steps.
What am I?

Answer: A slide.

Alan Zyamunt (7)
Queen Mary Avenue Infant School, Cleethorpes

A Hero Riddle

I live in the sewers.
My colour is green.
I have swords.
I wear a blue bandanna.
I have brothers.
I have a master.
Who am I?

Answer: Leonardo - Ninja Turtle.

Joshua Farrar (7)
Queen Mary Avenue Infant School, Cleethorpes

A Winged Creature

I can fly high.
I have wings.
I am colourful.
I eat tasty bugs.
You can see me in the summer.
I start life as a caterpillar.
What am I?

Answer: A butterfly.

Laila Campbell (6)
Queen Mary Avenue Infant School, Cleethorpes

An Insect Riddle

I am very small.
I have wings that are fast.
I have lots of eyes.
I can fly high.
Spiders catch me on their web.
Spiders eat me.
What am I?

Answer: A fly.

Brogan Lawson (6)
Queen Mary Avenue Infant School, Cleethorpes

Monster Creature

I have white, sharp teeth.
I have a pointy fin.
I have a blue body.
I live in the ocean.
I am fast and strong.
I eat fish.
What am I?

Answer: A shark.

Callum Hooper (6)
Queen Mary Avenue Infant School, Cleethorpes

Scaredy Cat

I have sharp claws.
I have sharp teeth.
I am frightened.
I live in Oz.
I would like some courage to make me brave.
Who am I?

Answer: *The Cowardly Lion.*

Dougie Brennan (6)
Queen Mary Avenue Infant School, Cleethorpes

Tree Creature

I am little.
I am spiky on my back.
I have sharp teeth that are little.
I eat flies.
I live in trees.
I am scaly.
What am I?

Answer: A lizard.

Ewan Conchar (7)
Queen Mary Avenue Infant School, Cleethorpes

Magical Creature

I have a magical horn.
I am fluffy and white.
I am enchanted.
I eat magical stuff.
I live in a wonderful forest.
What am I?

Answer: A unicorn.

Jayden Webster-Olley (7)
Queen Mary Avenue Infant School, Cleethorpes

Pink Tentacled Monster

I don't have a brain.
I am in different colours.
I live in the sea,
And I live in groups.
I can sting you.
What am I?

Answer: A jellyfish.

Amelia Erin Rayne-Beau Byram (7)
Queen Mary Avenue Infant School, Cleethorpes

Tail Whacker

I am small but my tail is long.
I live in Australia.
I am green and grey.
I have some claws.
I have a tiny body.
What am I?

Answer: A lizard.

Riley Noble (6)
Queen Mary Avenue Infant School, Cleethorpes

The Stomper

I stomp around.
I hunt for food.
I roar.
I have sharp teeth.
I eat meat.
What am I?

Answer: A T-rex.

Bailey Jay Taylor-Dunham (7)
Queen Mary Avenue Infant School, Cleethorpes

On A Hill

I am tall.
My gates are dark.
I am grey,
But sometimes I am colourful.
I have a posh room.
My favourite place is a secret place.
I have lots of people living in me.
I don't make a noise.
What am I?

Answer: A castle.

Martha Piercey (7)
Seathorne Primary School, Skegness

The Fast Winner

I have two handlebars for hands.
I go on the twisty road.
I need fuel for my body.
I have two tyres,
One at the back and one at the front.
I have an engine.
I go really fast on the road.
What am I?

Answer: A motorbike.

Kayden Hodgson (7)
Seathorne Primary School, Skegness

The Big, Blue Creature

I live underneath the dark, scary water.
I can't breathe very well under water.
I am a fabulous, gigantic underwater creature.
I am as big as six double-deckers.
I live in the hottest seas.
What am I?

Answer: A whale.

Lexie Frost (7)
Seathorne Primary School, Skegness

I Am A Giant

I breathe over the shallow sea.
I eat delicious, scrumptious fish for my tea.
I turn when I breathe over the ocean.
I'm blue and white like the icy sea.
When I breathe, I make a big splash.
What am I?

Answer: A whale.

Jaxon Young (6)
Seathorne Primary School, Skegness

The High Flyer

I feel as soft as a bear.
I look like a beautiful, colourful bird.
I collect teeth from people.
I have lots of money.
I have two wings like a bird flying.
I live in a lovely place.
What am I?

Answer: A tooth fairy.

Emily Boyle (7)
Seathorne Primary School, Skegness

Something Scrumptious

I can melt like an ice cube.
I can be as white as snow.
I can be brown like thin gravy.
Kids really like me like sweets.
Sometimes I am as hard as rock.
My shape can be a snowman.
What am I?

Answer: Chocolate.

Nico Gedney (6)
Seathorne Primary School, Skegness

The Green Waver

I am green like small, thin grass.
I wave about like swaying flowers in the wind.
I live in the vast, sapphire sea.
You find me in the fantastic seabed.
Some ferocious creatures eat me.
What am I?

Answer: Seaweed.

Charlie Webb (7)
Seathorne Primary School, Skegness

I Look Beautiful

I am colourful like white,
Blue, pink and purple.
I wave about sometimes.
I have fantastic colours.
My colours look beautiful,
Like someone dressed in a pretty dress.
What am I?

Answer: A flower.

Ellie Manley (7)
Seathorne Primary School, Skegness

Under The Sparkling Sea

I like colourful, beautiful shells.
I can swim beautifully.
I am a good swimmer.
I can go under the dark, blue sea.
I have a lovely palace.
I have long, red hair.
Who am I?

Answer: A mermaid.

Evie Lily Beale (7)
Seathorne Primary School, Skegness

What Am I?

I turn into spikes.
I have a little, cute face.
I am as spiky as pins.
I have very small and pretty legs.
I am as shiny as a jewel.
I am as small as a ruler.
What am I?

Answer: A hedgehog.

Summer Louise Turner (7)
Seathorne Primary School, Skegness

The Sweet, Unhealthy, Cold Food

You will need me on a nice,
Hot, summer's day.
People like eating me,
But they might get a brain freeze.
I melt in the sun.
I am very delicious.
What am I?

Answer: Ice cream.

Lilli Mitchell (6)
Seathorne Primary School, Skegness

The Loud Roarer

I live in the latest Cretaceous period.
I fight a spinosaurus.
I eat meat.
I roar loud like a lion.
I'm green like the meadow waving in the wind.
What am I?

Answer: A T-rex.

Kainan Brooks (7)
Seathorne Primary School, Skegness

The Tree Climber

I live in the deep forest.
I am ginger.
I can climb green trees.
I am surrounded by tall trees.
I am small.
I have a tail like a skunk.
What am I?

Answer: A squirrel.

Grace Gathercole (7)
Seathorne Primary School, Skegness

What Am I?

I am like a red hot sun.
I am orange.
I have orange skin.
Some people eat me.
I have seeds.
I have very wet skin.
I live on trees.
What am I?

Answer: An orange.

Jacob Blythe (7)
Seathorne Primary School, Skegness

The Flying Thing

I quack like a duck.
I swim in a blue river.
I make cute babies.
I fly high in the sky.
I flap my wings.
Sometimes I go on the grass.
What am I?

Answer: A goose.

Borys Chojnacki (6)
Seathorne Primary School, Skegness

In The Sea

I have sharp teeth,
And I live in the sea.
I'm blue like the sky.
I'm in the deep, blue sea,
And I am blue like the sea.
What am I?

Answer: A shark.

Maisie Ladds (7)
Seathorne Primary School, Skegness

The Deep Diver

I live in the deep, blue sea.
I am blue like the bright, sapphire sky.
I have one big, blue fin on my back.
I have two on my sides.
What am I?

Answer: A dolphin.

Lilith Scarlet Thompson (7)
Seathorne Primary School, Skegness

What Am I?

I am as blue as the bright, sapphire sky.
I wave a lot.
I have rare animals in me.
I turn white in the frightening, bright storm.
What am I?

Answer: The ocean.

Riley Hale (6)
Seathorne Primary School, Skegness

A High Flyer

I have lumpy skin on my legs.
I have sharp nails on my feet.
My wings go straight when I fly.
I eat people's ice creams.
What am I?

Answer: A bird.

Amelia Rose Holmes (7)
Seathorne Primary School, Skegness

A High Hopper

I have four really wobbly legs.
I live in the very dark wood.
I am soft like the white snow.
I eat crunchy carrots.
What am I?

Answer: A rabbit.

Lilly-Mai Allan (6)
Seathorne Primary School, Skegness

A High Flyer

I have big, strong wings.
I fly in the twinkly, shiny, blue sky.
I have red-hot breath.
I am as green as the grass.
What am I?

Answer: A dragon.

Lily-Beth Ellen Brader (7)
Seathorne Primary School, Skegness

In The Grass

I live in the wavy, short grass.
I like moving in the short grass.
I move very slowly.
I never talk.
What am I?

Answer: A worm.

Chloe Carey (7)
Seathorne Primary School, Skegness

Sharp Teeth

I live in the sparkling, sapphire sea.
I have sharp teeth.
I have big, black gills.
I am grey.
What am I?

Answer: A shark.

Jacobi-Joe Welbourn (7)
Seathorne Primary School, Skegness

What Am I?

I jump around.
I have sharp claws.
I am white.
I have a white tail.
I have goofy teeth.
What am I?

Answer: A rabbit.

Noah Howe (7)
Seathorne Primary School, Skegness

The Riddle Of The Loud Roar

I am orange.
I run fast.
I have a long tail.
I have a fluffy coat.
I have brown ears.
What am I?

Answer: A cat.

Kyra Feeley (6)
Seathorne Primary School, Skegness

The Spiky Animal

I turn into a ball.
I have spikes on my back.
I have a small nose.
I have black eyes.
What am I?

Answer: A hedgehog.

Daniel Luke Stephenson (7)
Seathorne Primary School, Skegness

What Am I?

I am soft and I jump high.
I drink water.
I jump.
I am furry.
I chase dogs.
What am I?

Answer: A cat.

Chelsie Lyn Taylor (7)
Seathorne Primary School, Skegness

I Am Really Fast

I am black,
And I eat meat.
I have four rough, small legs.
I have fast legs.
What am I?

Answer: A T-rex.

Cooper Rolfe (6)
Seathorne Primary School, Skegness

A Fast Speed

I have red legs.
I run as fast as possible.
I am red.
I am a superhero.
Who am I?

Answer: Flash Gordon.

Brooklyn Whitworth (6)
Seathorne Primary School, Skegness

What Am I?

I have sharp claws.
I have sharp teeth.
I have a long tail.
I am brown.
What am I?

Answer: A cat.

Alfie Thomson (7)
Seathorne Primary School, Skegness

What Am I?

I can swing.
I can eat bananas.
I sleep.
I look like an animal.
What am I?

Answer: A monkey.

Wyatt Senior (7)
Seathorne Primary School, Skegness

The Hot Oven

I am as hot as an oven.
I am boiling hot.
I am bright and dazzling.
What am I?

Answer: The sun.

Sophie Clarke (6)
Seathorne Primary School, Skegness

A High Flyer

I go really fast.
I go low and high.
I fly in the sky.
What am I?

Answer: A jet.

Preston Wilkinson (6)
Seathorne Primary School, Skegness

A Super High Jump

I swim really fast.
I swim in the ocean.
I am blue.
What am I?

Answer: A shark.

Jayden Dylan Senanayake-Andrew (7)
Seathorne Primary School, Skegness

What Am I?

I am brown.
I am fluffy.
I can run.
I am big.
What am I?

Answer: A horse.

Teyen Wood (6)
Seathorne Primary School, Skegness

The Silver, Sharp Tooth

I have a very long, pink tail.
I have giant whiskers.
I am bright silver.
I have got mini legs.
I have a silver tummy,
With a bit of purple as well.
I have orange on my face,
And I have some blue ears with pink in the middle.
I only eat yellow cheese with holes.
What am I?

Answer: A mouse.

Maisie Wallis (7)
Wragby Primary School, Wragby

The Red-Hot Smoking Beast

I am big and fierce.
I have spikes on my back,
And wings as big as a building.
I have big, stomping feet that are loud.
I am very big.
I am the biggest creature in the land,
And the world.
Everyone is scared of me.
Nobody should like me.
What am I?

Answer: A dragon.

David-Malakai Kuyava (6)
Wragby Primary School, Wragby

The Mysterious Shadow

I have pink, glittering hair.
I have rainbow skin.
I'm as beautiful as glitter.
I'm nearly as fast as a cheetah.
My hooves are as shiny as gold.
My horn is as shiny as silver.
What am I?

Answer: A unicorn.

Daniel Blood (7)
Wragby Primary School, Wragby

The Gingery Orange

I have incredible stripes on my back.
I have orange fur.
I have a long, swishy tail.
I have long, sharp claws.
I am like a cat.
I get ready when I see a bird,
Or a mouse.
What am I?

Answer: A tiger.

Gracie Lowe (6)
Wragby Primary School, Wragby

The Fiery Beast

I have sharp spikes on my back.
I am as red as fire.
I have sharp teeth.
I live in a smoky den.
I am bigger than a hose.
I am scared of mice.
What am I?

Answer: A dragon.

Noah Pearce (6)
Wragby Primary School, Wragby

The Cute Animal

Sometimes I live in water.
I have a bumpy shell.
I can swim in water.
I have big eyes.
I have a wide mouth.
I eat tiny fish.
What am I?

Answer: A turtle.

Sophie Olivia Millington (6)
Wragby Primary School, Wragby

The Big Beast

I am flying really high.
I am as red as a brick.
I have sharp teeth.
I am scary.
I've got a spiky tail.
I hate mice.
What am I?

Answer: A dragon.

Ben Spencer (7)
Wragby Primary School, Wragby

The Small Runner

I run in my cage.
I am furry.
I nibble on grapes.
I have a small tail.
I like to hide in fine straw.
I like to sleep.
What am I?

Answer: A hamster.

Evie Deans (6)
Wragby Primary School, Wragby

The Cute Pet

I am fluffy.
I have sharp teeth.
I am kind.
I am dark black.
I have a tail which is wiggly.
I am bigger than a fish.
What am I?

Answer: A dog.

Amy Chamberlain (6)
Wragby Primary School, Wragby

Dangerous Beast

I have old, fluffy fur.
I am as fast as a cheetah.
I love going forwards in the field,
And around the fire station.
What am I?

Answer: A fierce dog.

Archie Mark Angél Rushin (6)
Wragby Primary School, Wragby

The Ginger Fur

I have soft fur.
I eat tiny mice.
I drink cold milk.
I sleep a lot.
I curl up like a ball.
I jump in the air.
What am I?

Answer: A cat.

Riley Joseph Spittles (6)
Wragby Primary School, Wragby

The Sharp Tooth

I have a fin.
I have gills.
I have sharp teeth.
I have a tail.
I have blue skin.
I have black eyes.
What am I?

Answer: A shark.

Zac Garth (6)
Wragby Primary School, Wragby

What Am I?

I have got a fluffy tail.
I am bright orange.
I have colourful fur.
I have a sharp tail.
What am I?

Answer: A tiger.

Thomas Blyth (6)
Wragby Primary School, Wragby

The Zebra Eater

I am fearless.
I eat meat.
I like zebra.
I have a fluffy tail.
I'll eat you.
What am I?

Answer: A lion.

Taya Nganga (6)
Wragby Primary School, Wragby

The Fluffy Friend

I live in a basket.
I eat fish and mice.
I have sharp claws.
I have green eyes.
What am I?

Answer: A black cat.

Thomas Skellern (7)
Wragby Primary School, Wragby

The Brown Rock

I have a brown shell on my back.
I walk very slowly.
I am as slow as a snail.
What am I?

Answer: A turtle.

Charlotte Wallis (7)
Wragby Primary School, Wragby

My Fluffy Friend

I am very cheeky.
I am so fluffy.
I have green eyes.
What am I?

Answer: A puppy.

Phoebe Cooper (7)
Wragby Primary School, Wragby

The Colourful Shadow

I have feathers.
I have two legs.
I eat crackers.
What am I?

Answer: A parrot.

Madeline Wade (7)
Wragby Primary School, Wragby

The Black Fluffball

I am fluffy.
I have whiskers.
I am black.
What am I?

Answer: A cat.

Ethen Hook-Bingham (6)
Wragby Primary School, Wragby

Est.1991

YOUNG WRITERS INFORMATION

We hope you have enjoyed reading this book – and that you will continue to in the coming years.

If you're a young writer who enjoys reading and creative writing, or the parent of an enthusiastic poet or story writer, do visit our website **www.youngwriters.co.uk**. Here you will find free competitions, workshops and games, as well as recommended reads, a poetry glossary and our blog.

If you would like to order further copies of this book, or any of our other titles, then please give us a call or visit **www.youngwriters.co.uk**.

Young Writers
Remus House
Coltsfoot Drive
Peterborough
PE2 9BF
(01733) 890066
info@youngwriters.co.uk